The Fence

The Art Of Protection

Geoff Thompson

SUMMERSDALE

Summersdale Publishers Ltd
46 West Street
Chichester
West Sussex
PO19 1RP
United Kingdom

www.summersdale.com

Photographs by David W Monks
Member of the Master Photographer's Association
Snappy Snaps Portrait Studio
7 Cross Cheaping
Coventry
CV1 1HF

Printed and bound in Great Britain.

ISBN 1 84024 084 9

About the Author

Geoff Thompson has written over 20 published books and is known world wide for his autobiographical books Watch My back, Bouncer and On The Door, about his nine years working as a night club doorman. He holds the rank of 5th Dan black belt in Japanese karate, 1st Dan in Judo and is also qualified to senior instructor level in various other forms of wrestling and martial arts. He has several scripts for stage, screen and TV in development with Destiny Films.

He has published several articles for GQ magazine, and has also been featured in FHM, Maxim, Arena, Front and Loaded magazines, and has been featured many times on mainstream TV.

Geoff is currently a contributing editor for Men's Fitness magazine and self defence columnist for Front.

Other books and videos by Geoff Thompson

Watch My Back – A Bouncer's Story
Bouncer (sequel to *Watch My Back*)
On the Door – *Further Bouncer Adventures.*
The Pavement Arena – *Adapting Combat Martial Arts to the Street*
Real Self-defence
Real Grappling
Real Punching
Real Kicking
Real Head, Knees & Elbows
Dead Or Alive – *Self-protection*
3 Second Fighter – The Sniper Option
Weight Training – For the Martial Artist
Animal Day
     – Pressure Testing the Martial Arts
Tuxedo Warrior: *Tales of a Mancunian Bouncer*, by Cliff Twemlow,
foreword by Geoff Thompson
Fear – The Friend of Exceptional People: techniques in controlling fear
Blue Blood on the Mat by Athol Oakley, foreword by Geoff Thompson
Give Him To The Angels
     – *The Story Of Harry Greb* by James R Fair

The Ground Fighting Series (books):
Vol. One   – Pins, the Bedrock
Vol. Two   – Escapes
Vol. Three   – Chokes and Strangles
Vol. Four   – Arm Bars and Joint Locks
Vol. Five   – Fighting From Your Back
Vol. Six   – Fighting From Neutral Knees

Videos:
Lessons with Geoff Thompson
Animal Day – Pressure Testing the Martial Arts
Animal Day Part Two   – The Fights
Three Second Fighter   – The Sniper Option
Throws and Take-Downs Vols. 1-6
Real Punching Vols. 1-3
The Fence

The Ground Fighting Series (videos):
Vol. One   – Pins, the Bedrock
Vol. Two   – Escapes
Vol. Three   – Chokes and Strangles
Vol. Four   – Arm Bars and Joint Locks
Vol. Five   – Fighting From Your Back
Vol. Six   – Fighting From Neutral Knees

Advanced Ground Fighting Vols. 1-3
Pavement Arena Part 1
Pavement Arena Part 2
        – The Protection Pyramid
Pavement Arena Part 3
        – Grappling, The Last Resort
Pavement Arena Part 4
        – Fit To Fight

Contents

Introduction

I worked the doors in Coventry for over nine years, and in that time encountered just about every malevolent, un-sentient being you can imagine. Their one goal in life – at least it appeared – was to make a hole in the ground with my head. This wouldn't be so bad if the very same people didn't want to hug and kiss me to oblivion every Christmas and New Year. I'm labouring the point, what I'm trying to say is that, after nine years of dealing with shit, I learned the best way to shovel. Without doubt my greatest physical development in all those years of neutralising violence was 'the fence'. I can't really say that I invented the fence because many people were, and are, already inadvertently using it successfully. What I can say is that I brought it to the forefront and categorised it.

Recognising the potency of this devastating, yet simple, technique, I developed it into an art form, so that many others who perhaps have less experience in the world of brutality might adopt it as a life-saving technique for the contemporary world of 'in your face' violence. I have to say that, conceptually, the fence is simple and anyone, irrespective of their skill level, can adopt it.

In most aspects of our life where a problem might present itself, simplicity is usually the answer, but often it is grossly overlooked because of its modest demeanour. The fence is no different; it is so real and so obvious that only the enlightened few seem to be able to see it. Many, it would appear, are looking up their own backsides for some mystical, complex, aesthetic dance routine that might devastate several opponents with a flick or a trip, and – at the same time – endear them to their peers. To the latter I would say 'stick to the kung fu movies because that's the only place it'll work.'

Sir Winston Churchill once said that many people stumble upon the truth and then get back up and wander off as though nothing had happened. And that's generally because the truth is often too simple – or it hurts – or it might mean too many changes. In short the truth is not palatable, it strikes at the heart of lost souls and forces them, momentarily, to see just how far astray they are. At face value the fence looks so simple that many people fail to see it's potency. It's not pretty enough to go into the curriculum of the majority who collect techniques like football cards. I don't collect ornaments to be displayed, I collect rocks that can be thrown at malevolents who wish to enter my world.

So, from the off, please try to look below the surface of the fence and take the word of a man that has used it very successfully in thousands of threatening and potentially threatening situations. This is the real deal – it's the tread on a fast tyre, the control before the power. The fence is where I spend most of my time when I train for reality. And as you'll see, as and when you begin to train in the fence, it is not quite as easy to put into practice as it looks.

The main reason why the fence will probably be the most important physical technique that you will learn is its controlling factor in a live scenario. As we should all know, control comes before power. Being the best puncher in the world, or the fastest kicker is of little use if you do not possess that pivotal ingredient 'control'.

To save any confusion I think I should reverse up and talk a little about the common misconceptions about street violence and how to train for it. Most people's idea of self-defence is either a match fight where two fighters 'have it' on the common, or they think it's the old 'block-counter' scenario. Not so I'm afraid, in both cases. So what kind of fighting do you train for? What kind of enemy are you preparing to fight? What are his weaknesses and his strengths? What are his limitations? Where is his layer? One thing is for sure you are very unlikely to meet up with anyone that throws attacks at you like they do in you martial arts class, that's why many of the techniques you develop in the controlled arena fail to work outside.

From my perspective, as an empiricist, I see combat as falling into 4 categories. I see basic self-defence/protection as being primarily about avoidance, escape, verbal dissuasion and, if all else has fails, a pre-emptive attack on your assailant – then run for your life. No hanging around to 'finish the opponent off', as is so often taught in unlikely self-defence classes all around the world. Hit and run – no more, no less. Then we have match fighting, which, as I explained earlier, is the scenario where we have an arranged fight on the common (very honourable but from a bygone age). When was the last time you saw two men with enough bottle to have a square go? It hardly ever happens. In the UFC (Ultimate Fight Competition) and other extreme fighting contests we see expert match fighters battling it out to discover who, and what style is potentate. But as honourable as this type of fighting may be we mustn't mistake it for street defence in this era. Then there is ambush fighting. Basically if you are switched off to the environment and to the contemporary enemy every fight/situation that you find yourself involved in will be a veritable ambush fight. Last, but not by any mean least we have the most contemporary fighting arena of the day. Three second fighting is where it is at, right now, on this ever-spinning planet that we inhabit.

Three second fighting is so called because most real fights do not go beyond three seconds in today's arena. It is cutting edge fighting where honour, unfortunately, has no place and the attackers leading technique is dialogue, using deception and distraction to secure destruction. The majority of fights in our age are either ambush fights, because most victims are switched off most of the time or three second fights, which start with some kind of dialogue. Of course we would be silly not to prepare for all types of fighting but we would be sillier still if we, like so many present day martial artists, prepare for none at all and just hope that our sparring practice will adequately prepare us.

At the risk of offending people out there (something that I don't want to do but inadvertently seem to anyway), I say 'WAKE UP!' If it's real combat you want then drop the flowers and start picking up the rocks. And please, whatever you do, don't take my word for any of this. Just pick up the newspapers, watch the TV news, open you eyes next time it kicks off in the club, the pub, outside the chippy and ask yourself one question 'will what I train in – my art – fit into that?' If it won't – or even if there is a little doubt – why won't it and why aren't you changing your art right now so that it does?

If you are outside the chippy with your lady or your kids and it kicks off, will your art, or more specifically the way that you train your art, stand up to the rigours of such naked aggression, when two ugly youths are in your face and screaming 'HAVE YOU GOT A ****ING PROBLEM WITH ME?!'

Forget the honour, the touch of gloves, the bows, the whistles and the etiquette. Forget what works in sparring or on the bag or even in the ring – they are different arenas. I don't care how big you are or how hard you hit – if you can't cope with that three seconds before it 'kicks off' and the consequences of what that fight entails – comebacks, police involvement, killing, being killed, threats to your life, your family etc – then all the talent in the world isn't going to help you. If you don't understand the contemporary enemy and that, in his world, deception is fair play, he is going to take you out of the game before you even realise that you are in it. And you can complain as much as you like about how unfair it all is and that you wouldn't have lost if he hadn't have hit you when you weren't looking but none of it will mean shit because you still lost and he still won. And losing in this environment does not mean a second place trophy, it may mean a hospital bed, or even your own slab at the city morgue. If you doubt me have a look in today's papers, or yesterday's or even tomorrow's and you will see written proof that death is a usual consequence of 'coming in second'. Sun Tzu had it right 25 centuries ago, understand the enemy, understand yourself, one hundred battles without fear of defeat.

The Fence

I have fought many skilled fighters in the street, some with better credentials than myself, others with over 20 years of martial spontaneity built into their brains. The majority I beat with a single technique. How? I switched off their spontaneity, I closed down their 20 years of experience, I made them novices again by taking them outside their own arena and using dialogue as my entry, deception as my 'trap' and a practised right hook as my coup de grace. I might feign cowardice by allowing them a peep at my fear, this feeds their confidence until it is fat and overripe. I'll ask them a question to engage their brain, creating a window of entry for my physical technique, then it is over before it has really begun.

I know that this would not work in the match fight arena against the fighters from the UFC etc. But hey, I can live with that because it is not the arena that I am threatened with in society. It is an arena that one only ever enters by choice, I don't need to prepare for that, I need to prepare for the arena that is forced upon me – the pavement arena. In the extreme fighting you develop match fighting skills to defeat other martial artists, outside it is, as they say, a horse of a completely different colour.

In the match fighting arena the grapplers generally win over. I admire them greatly, I train in grappling, but do I really want to be grappling outside a bar? I don't think so. Many of my friends have made this mistake and been hurt, one killed, for their blunder. Two of my friends were stabbed by women whilst they grappled on the floor with men. If you have ever faced more than one opponent in a street situation then you will know that grappling is the very last place you want to go. My intention here is not to be disrespectful to the grappling or martial arts fraternity, and if anyone is offended there is no need to write in and say so, because I offer my apology here and now. I know that training in all ranges is pivotal if you want to be a complete and rounded martial artist. But as a man who has 'had it' in the street more times that I care to remember, I owe it to the reader to be completely honest and tell it as I see it. What kind of a teacher, or man would I be if I wasn't honest.

For a lot of people 3second fighting still hasn't sunk in. This is absolutely scandalous because we all secretly know that this is where it's at. Maybe we're not all ready to hear it yet on a conscious level, but it's true and it's about time we all got ready for it. Three second fighting should be taught to every self-respecting martial artist on the planet – it should be pivotal on every curriculum.

Three second fighting is where dialogue is used to attack and prime – and very often defeat – an attacker, and where the concept of defence (the block/counter variety) is about as useful as a castor sugar jet ski. If you don't attack first in this arena, and I mean in a hurry, you will get attacked and attacked and attacked, and if your wife or your mother or your child dares to try and stop the frenzied assault they'll got some too. Forget the films! This is real life! If you're not first then you're second, and on the pavement arena second is a very sorry last.

Of course, if you survive you can go to the police in the aftermath, but all that'll do is add another year of intense, ulcer-inducing, sleep-destroying, life-sapping worry to the physical scars that you already carry. Your life will go on hold for this length of time. Many find that they have to move to a different district because the scum that they are taking to court do not take kindly to being informed upon. I am not saying don't go to the police, I am simply saying don't expect them to solve all your problems because I doubt that they will.

A skirmish outside the chippy, if you do not assume control and take these people out of their league may, and probably will, change the course of your life – especially if you are not used to dealing in the currency that we so flippantly refer to as violence. This is where the fence comes into its own, in that it allows you to control a situation in the early stages of dialogue. If you find yourself unable to talk your way out of a situation the fence also allows you to attack from your controlling stance and destroy every threat in you path.

Again I should regress here and tell you that my own personal belief is that you should walk away from violence whenever and however you can. Most situations can be avoided if you have a small ego and a big awareness. Those that cannot be avoided can usually be escaped, again only if you have the control of your ego. Dissuasion is very good for talking down those situations that have not been avoided or escaped but you may have to 'appear' to swallow your pride a little for this to be completely effective. If you are very confident with your art and its workability in the street you will be able to walk away with confidence knowing that you are letting the other fellow off. If however you are not so confident all the more reason to swallow and walk away, if the other fellow will allow you to.

Of course, we are living in a callous society that does not look kindly on those that walk away from confrontations; the enemy is often cruel and despotic and seems to enjoy attacking for little or no reason. We are then placed in a position where, with the best will and intention in the world, we will not be able to walk away, we either attack or get attacked, whether we be the hammer or the anvil.

That's where this text will come into its own, in that it will prepare you for this pivotal moment so that you can defend yourself and your loved ones without even dropping your chips.

The Fence

Depending upon when you read this text, it is now July of the year 1998, it too may already be antiquated, a new environment and a new enemy may already have forced yet another paradigm shift in the art of defence (no doubt many will still have not changed from the first time around?!). If a change has occurred, then your duty to yourself and those that you wish to protect is to take this metaphoric, old piece of cloth and re-tailor it so that it fits. Nothing is lost, nothing is a wasted – some things just don't fit the way they should and many of the martial arts fashion victims of the 1990s refuse to get vogue, even though it may save their lives.

So many people are fighting ghosts, samurai on horseback, enemies that have died decades before. We should take the advice of the great poet William Blake and 'drive our cart and our plow over the bones of the dead.' In other words let's take our lessons from the past, but be sure not to carry their bones on our backs like an ever ladening burden. Take the techniques from this text and please make them your own. The way they are set out in this book is the way that suits me and some of the experienced fighters that I have known. However we are not you, and we are all intrinsically different so you should alter the techniques herein so that they fit you as a person. Cloning should be outlawed in the martial arts and all of our arts should look a little different if they are going to work for us as individuals in this multi-faceted, ever evolving society.

Have fun with the book and the techniques and above all be a nice person – karma is always kinder to nice people.

Chapter One

The Premise

In this book we are working on the premise that, if a street confrontation occurs, you have already exhausted all other options, i.e. avoidance, escape, verbal dissuasion, loopholing and posturing. Most self-defence situations and attack scenarios issue rays of prior warning, if you are perceptive enough to spot the attackers ritual. If you are foolhardy enough to heighten your vulnerability by placing yourself in a dangerous situation (walking down a dark alley at night etc) you cannot expect any prior warning and will have to make the best of a bad situation. You then fall into the 'ambush attack' scenario. Most people in society are so switched off, both mentally and environmentally, that many attack scenarios fall into this category. If this is the case – and it so often is – then you will be fighting tooth and nail for your very existence. The majority will not survive the ambush attack purely because they have never trained for it.

Previously I talked about the verbal communication that often precedes an attack upon the person and the victim who is quite often disarmed or shocked rigid by it, The time lapse between the disarming, or scarifying verbal (which can be very short) and the attack itself is 'your time'. During these seconds you may 'seize the moment', as it were, and be pre-emptive, effecting attack or/and escape. Alternatively you can elongate the verbal by replying to the aforementioned dialogue with submissive or aggressive counter-verbal. These seconds before battle are absolutely pivotal. They must be managed quickly and without demur; remember, hesitancy begets defeat. This arena is that of the 3 second fighter.

When the police talk about self-protection the key word is 'target hardening' that is, making yourself a hard target by means of placement and awareness of environment and the enemy. When I talk about the physical aspect of self-protection I am always working on the premise that, for whatever reason, a situation has gone beyond this and reached dire straits and the possibility of escape is no longer an option.

As I have just said pre-fight management is vital if you want to survive intact, the winner and loser in most situations is usually determined by what happens pre-fight as opposed to in-fight. Most situations start at conversation range, this being talking or hand shake distance, if this is mismanaged it degenerates very quickly to vertical grappling range and then ground fighting – not a good place to be if you don't know the arena or are facing more than one opponent. Whilst we can't really choose the range we want to fight at in the street, it is usually thrust upon us, we can maintain it so that it doesn't degenerate further

The Fence

into grappling range by 'putting a fence around our factory'.

If you had a factory that you wanted to protect from robbers, the most sensible thing to do would be to place a fence around it, to make it a hard target. A potential robber has then got to get past that fence before he can even think about attacking the factory. Whilst the fence might not keep him out indefinitely it will make his job decidedly harder. This is rather like a boxer who constantly flicks a jab in front of his opponent's face. Even if that jab does not hit his opponent, it still keeps him at bay, and if his opponent wants to employ his knock out blow, he first has to find away past his opponent's jab. To the boxer the jab is the fence around his factory.

In self-protection the fence around your factory is your lead hand, placed in that all-important space between you and your antagonist to maintain a safe gap. Like the factory fence the lead hand will not keep an aggressor at bay forever – just long enough for you to initiate an escape or a pre-emptive attack – but it will place you in charge, even though your aggressor may not know it. Placed correctly, the lead hand and reverse hand will not only maintain a safe gap, but it will also disable the attackers armoury – right and left hand techniques/ head butt etc (though he may not know it on a conscious level, he will instinctively realise that until that fence has been removed or by-passed, his techniques have no clear way through).

The Fence

Sensory tentacle

The lead hand acts as a sensory tentacle (be very careful how you say this when you've had a few drinks, it could get you a slap across the face from the barmaid!) to your aggressor's intentions and should be held in a non-aggressive way. It should not touch the aggressor unless he makes a forward movement and tries to bridge the gap between you and he. If he does move forward he will touch the fence and set your alarm bells ringing – this forward movement should be checked so as to maintain the safe range by using the palm of the lead hand on the aggressor's chest. Don't hold the touch as this may be seen by your assailant, on a conscious level, as a controlling movement (whilst of course it is a controlling action, it's better at this stage that the aggressor does not feel that you are in control), which may create a power play and force him to knock your hand away or grab your wrist or even cause him to attack you prematurely. As soon as you have checked him, return the lead hand to its stand-by position.

One of the final precursors to an aggressor's attack is distance close down. If the antagonist tries to bridge the gap that you are maintaining, it is usually because he is making his final preparations for assault. So, if he moves forward and touches the fence you should, as well as checking range, be getting ready to attack pre-emptively or posture – or suffer the consequences should he break down the fence. In my opinion, the maximum number of times that a potential attacker should be allowed to touch the 'fence' is twice – after that you've got big problems and will probably end up in a match fight situation or on the floor with a crowd around you, depending up on the calibre of fighter you are facing. Every time the attacker touches the fence the danger doubles.

The 'fence' should look and feel natural, this will come with practice. If it doesn't appear natural and the attacker notices it on a conscious level, he will try to knock it away and bridge the gap – ideally the 'fence' should look like you are using your hands to talk ('talking hands' as my friend Maurice (Mo) Teague calls it).

A professional may notice the 'fence' no matter how well you disguise it and try using deceptive dialogue or body language to bring the 'fence' down – once he succeeds he will act. This often entails telling you that he does not want trouble, or that he just wants to talk, he may ask you for directions, ask the time, ask your name, anything to disarm you enough to lower the fence. An experienced fighter will offer to shake hands to get rid of the fence or try to close the gap by putting his arm around your shoulder in a pally kind of way – don't have any of it. If there is the slightest chance of threat then don't let anyone touch you – a good fighter will only need one shot once the fence is down, so keep it up.

The Fence

If he still persists in coming forward and you don't feel ready to strike, or indeed are not even sure that a strike is called for, don't hesitate to back up the 'check' with a firm verbal fence, 'Just stay where you are.'

With the modern enemy the rule of thumb is 'if his lips are moving he's lying' so don't believe a word that he says. If he still persists in coming forward then he has given you the 'go'. Having said all that, if the potential attacker has already made his intentions obvious by asking you for your wallet or threatening you then there is nothing to contemplate, you should 'go' the first time the touches the 'fence'.

Range finder

The fence also acts as a range finder. Many trained fighters misjudge the distance of their attacks in a real situation because the range is foreign to them. By touching the opponent with the lead hand before initiating your attack you can judge the correct striking distance, enabling you a more accurate and solid shot.

Action trigger

If and when you decide to initiate an attack, the lead hand also acts as a physical action trigger, you touch the opponent with the lead hand – find the range – and bounce off the touch using it to trigger your attack. This movement should be coupled with the verbal brain-engaging action trigger.

Multiple attackers

The 'fence' can also be used to maintain the range and even position of multiple attackers. However, because this is tantamount to fighting on more than one front, and it is very difficult to maintain the range of more than one attacker, a speedy decision to attack or escape should always be sought.

The fence can be constructed in any way you choose, as long as it blocks the gap between you and your adversary and looks inoffensive. You can use a 'stop fence' by placing the palm of the lead hand in front of the opponent, but this will bring the control to a conscious level and may catalyse alarm in your opponent – where possible it is best to control him without him knowing it.

Chapter Two

The Fence

The Pleading Fence (PF)

This is a nice fence because it is submissive and inoffensive but it blocks range brilliantly, it also leaves the fingers ideally placed for an eye attack should it be needed. It is often best to underline the fence with firm, but submissive dissuasive dialogue, 'look, just keep away from me, I don't want trouble' or a more assertive 'stay where you are – don't come any closer.'

Being submissive is ideal if you have decided that you are going to employ a pre-emptive attack or you are using the deception to escape, it will mentally disarm your opponent. However, this approach does have a down side: many attackers will see it as a meal ticket to an easy victim and this may spur on their assault. This reaction is OK if you are setting the trap, but not so good if you are not expecting it. Personally I use the submissive approach quite a lot because it really does disarm the opponent and give you a clear line for the sniper option attack, whereas at other times I will use an assertive, even aggression fence, to psyche out the opponent.

Assertiveness can be both a good and a bad thing. If your attacker thinks that you are confident, it may cause him to abort his intended attack – after all 'when ignorance is mutual, confidence is king'. However, if he is committed to attacking you no matter what, your assertiveness may trigger his aggression and you may lose the element of surprise and provide him with added adrenal turbo.

Having spent a lot of time working with and controlling violent people, I have learned to judge the right time for assertiveness and the right time for submissiveness. Not everyone will be able to do this, so, if you have a choice, use submissiveness to disarm and then attack and run, or use firm (but not aggressive) or submissive verbal dissuasion.

Both hands are placed in front of you, palms facing the attacker and several inches away from him but not touching.

The Staggered Fence (SF)

Similar to the PF with palms facing forward, but with the hands staggered by about one foot. The hand at the back would be the ideal one to use in attack, though with practice the lead hand would be ideally placed for a finger strike to the eyes.

The Exclamation Fence (EF)

The hands, palms upward, are held as though in exclamation, the lead left hand pushed forward as fence and the right hand, cocked to strike, to your own right hand side (left if reversed).

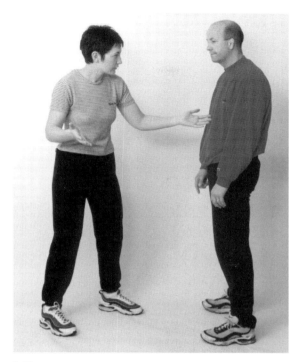

The Verbal Fence

The verbal fence is an excellent tool if you can see menace on its way in and works well pre-fight, in-fight and post-fight – I have used it successfully many times. This extract below from my book Bouncer exemplifies a post-fight fence rather well. The fight with the 'karate kid' had been on the cards for several months, I'd tried to avoid it but was unable. I pick up the situation as it reached its conclusion – the post-fight fence comes in at the end of the fight when one of his friends becomes involved (this was a match fight by the way).

'I'd spent two months trying to avoid this situation and was fed up with trying, I had no more chances left in my 'chance bag'.

As the karate kid got closer his face began to grimace and I sensed he was going to strike at any moment. 'BANG!' Almost in slow motion, I hooked my right fist onto his advancing jaw, pushing it backwards, shaking his grey matter into the realms of unconsciousness. As he fell I volleyed his face and he spiralled, like movie strobe. I kicked him so hard that it hurt my foot. I felt hate leaving my body; he landed face down and forlorn on the cruel, black tarmac of defeat. Many people were watching, so I thought I'd give them a display, not for exhibitionism, nor fun, nor ego, I just wanted to take out a little insurance. Making the onlookers (mostly his mates) think that I was an animal would, in the future, insure that they did not tangle with me. It's what the Chinese call 'killing a chicken to train a monkey'

'Kiaaa,' I screamed as I brought an axe kick onto the body of my sleeping quarry. To the onlooker, it probably looked barbaric (which is how I wanted it to look), but in reality the kick was empty, I pulled it on impact, just as I had a thousand times in training. The man with the weasel face (the karate kid's mate) ran at me, from the crowd of onlookers, with ill intent and I stopped him in his tracks with a lash of my tongue (the verbal fence).

'GER OUT 'F MY ****ING FACE BEFORE I DESTROY YA!'

I pointed at him to underline my resolve. He stopped like an insect on fly paper.'

Unlike the varying genres of physical fence the verbal fence is best aggressive – the more so the better. It needs to pierce the opponent's sub-conscious and register danger with the brain – thus causing an adrenal reaction in him that he will hopefully mistake for fear.

In America they have a saying in the prisons, 'Give me five feet', meaning, 'keep at least five feet away from me' – 5 feet being the distance that they feel they are relatively safe at. This only works if you are perceptive enough to spot menace at a very early stage. More often than not a fight will arise from an argument or some kind of aggressive verbal so the 5 feet rule is already lost and the physical fence comes into play.

If you are using the verbal fence you must, as I have said, be very firm, even aggressive;

'Stay where you are, don't come any closer, stay!'

This would be underlined by placing your lead hand in front of you in a stop sign. This tactic can even work in-fight if someone tries to attack you whilst you are fighting/defending yourself. I have been grappling on the floor with one opponent when his mate has tried to join in against me, noticing this I used an in-fight fence by telling the guy that if he joined in I was going to batter him afterwards – he quickly changed his mind.

The Fence

Conscious Physical Fence – Posturing

If you find yourself facing a potential attacker who is constantly touching the fence and giving you signs that his attack is imminent, but you can't bring yourself to attack pre-emptively, then you need to create a gap between you and him and take the fence to a conscious level (so that your opponent realises that you are taking control). If he is trying to bridge the gap and take down your fence, but you are not prepared to attack, then you MUST take the fence to a conscious level or you will face grave danger: the fence will be crushed and you attacked as a consequence.

It is important with the conscious fence to create a gap – about 5 feet would be good – between you and your opponent. You do this by stepping back, away from the attacker, whilst simultaneously using your lead hand to shove the attacker so that he also moves back. Creating this gap can also be done using a slap and step back, a two handed shove or a Thai leg kick. As long as, after the contact, you step back and create a gap between you and he. If you find that it is impossible to step back, perhaps your back is against a wall or something similar, then you should create a gap by pushing the antagonist back.

The intention of the sharp shove (or whatever device you use) is to trigger adrenalin in your opponent, thus hopefully triggering his 'flight response' (making him feel the urge to want to run away). So, if the situation has reached an impasse and you think it is going to become physical, but you do not want to pre-emptively attack him for whatever reason – then shove him hard on the chest so that it knocks him backwards and out of immediate attacking range. This minimal physical contact will cause an adrenal release in the opponent. Back the shove up with a very aggressive verbal fence like, 'Stay there, don't ****ing move!', using expletives to add intent and aggression.

The Fence

The reasons for the gap are manifold, not least because it takes the opponent out of his striking range. What it also does is take the opponent from a state of reaction to a state of response – from 'fight' response to 'flight' response. Let me explain: if you shove the opponent, but not out of range, he may automatically react to the shove with a counter-shove, or an attack, of his own. He'll do this without even thinking because it is an automatic reaction. Whilst in fight or flight mode we are in what is known as 'mid-brain', and in mid-brain we are hardly discernible from animals. Our prime objective in mid-brain is survival, and if that means running away that is what our instinct will get us to do. In effect, by staying within strike range you are forcing the opponent into a 'fight' response, and he will react like a cornered animal. His instincts (which will have been in his genes through many, many generations) will inform him that he is cornered and that he should 'fight his way out'. (This is not a good thing for obvious reasons.) If however you shove him out of attack range you will trigger his 'flight' response and give him the instinct to run or freeze because he is no longer a cornered animal, so there is no longer a reason to fight. He won't even know this on a conscious level, but thousands of years of instinct will inform him that he is no longer cornered and he should run for his very life. Even if he does not run away, the fact that he feels like running away will create confusion and self-doubt triggering more adrenaline and a downward spiral to capitulation.

The Fence

Once you have created a gap (and the confusion) the opponent is forced out of attack mode and into escape mode. The only way that he is going to be able to override this very strong emotion is to consciously disregard all natural instincts and move forward. Not an easy task, especially if the adversary is not an experienced one. This very often effects what I like to call the 'sticky feet syndrome'. The attacker may very well want to move forward because peer pressure demands that he fight and not run away, but his feet appear stuck to the floor, his body lurches forward as though trying to move, but his feet stay stuck firmly to the ground. This is because natural instinct is telling him to run for it.

Once you have created the gap make yourself a hard target by 'ballooning', or 'stalking'. This is done by pacing left to right without taking your eyes off the opponent, at the same time you shout out verbal commands like, 'stay there, don't move!' and point to the opponent, this acts as a secondary back up fence to the verbal.

Interestingly the ballooning also triggers innate instincts within the opponent that go right back to the dawn of mammalian man, when we were not at the top of the food chain and were prey to bigger animals. Your antagonist will literally feel as though he is being 'stalked' before attack. The thought that he is being hunted like a wild beast will serve to increase his woe. If you watch the cheetah when it hunts the antelope, he balloons (or stalks) just before the attack – in fact most animals do, we are no exception. It can be used by us as an attacking tool to trick the opponent into a flight response, or against us – often inadvertently – to effect the same 'freeze' or 'flight' tendencies.

You should back your ballooning up with a physical fence (pointing), and a verbal fence in the form of strong commands, 'keep away from me, stay where you are!' etc. If you make this display loud and aggressive and splay your arms erratically this would be classed as 'posturing' (which I will go into in great detail in my book *The Art of Fighting Without Fighting*). Basically though, 'posturing' is the art of fighting without fighting. It's what animals do in nature, generally with other animals of their own species. Rather than fight and kill each other and thus threaten the survival of their own species, they posture by making themselves as big and as aggressive as possible, to trigger the flight response in their opponent, defeating them without injury. I recommend that you take advantage of your opponent's reaction to your posturing and make your getaway as soon as possible.

The Psychological Fence
The psychological fence is a fighter's reputation or confident/aggressive gait – this places an invisible fence around you that only the very brave will try to pass.

The Fence

By walking tall and appearing fearless you put off many potential attackers who will not see you as a victim.

The Negative Psychological Fence

Deliberately dropping the physical or psychological fence by pretending to be scared or unthreatening can draw the opponent forward onto your intended attack – he walks into a trap. This is a good ploy for the very experienced player, but not one that I would recommend if you have not got heavy attacking artillery. In other words if you are going to use this technique to create an opening for your attack, first make sure that you know how to attack otherwise you fall in to the 'dog chasing the fire engine' category. If a dog chases a fire engine and suddenly catches it, he doesn't actually know what to do with it. Similarly, if you draw an opponent into an attack but don't have an effective attack prepared yourself, you are up shit creek.

The Invisible Fence

An experienced player will use what I call the invisible fence. That means he will have the confidence and experience to face an opponent without employing a physical fence. He knows his range and his enemy so well that he can sense when there will be movement and he can feel bad intent. If his opponent moves forward, he will move back or use a stop hit attack instinctively.

On the one hand the physical fence will control range and prime your attack, on the other, if you are not sure whether to strike or not, the fence allows you time to maintain a relatively safe zone whilst you plan a course of action. You need to bear in mind of course that decision-making this late in the game is not a good thing, although sometimes it is unavoidable.

Chapter Three

Action Trigger/Brain Engagement

An 'action trigger' is a word or sentence that you can use to trigger action. When facing potential menace it is very often difficult to initiate a physical attack, never quite knowing the right moment to 'go'. A key word or sentence will take away that decision-making. Your chosen word or sentence will automatically initiate your attack. Preferably you should use a submissive question, as opposed to a flat statement. This will serve the multi-purpose of switching off the opponent's adrenaline, brain engagement and action trigger. The submissive question is also a subliminal intimation to you antagonist that you wish to elongate conversation, whereas shorter sentences, certainly single syllables, send the message that conversation is coming to an end and a physical altercation is about to begin.

Whilst the flat statement, i.e., 'I don't want trouble', is submissive and can act as an action trigger it does not adequately engage the brain, because it does not demand an answer. Neither does it suggest that you wish to elongate the conversation. Even an abstract question can be multi-purpose, i.e., 'How did the City get on today?' because of the confusion factor, after all, what has the 'City result' got to do with the attacker wanting to punch your head in? Of course this all works nicely within the context of the four D's (dialogue, deception, distraction and destruction), your multi-faceted question being 'deception' and 'distraction' before the 'decision' of fight or flight. If the antagonist proffers a question you may wish your pre-emptive 'blurb' to be in the guise of an answer to it, or you may wish to feign deafness by saying, "Sorry mate, I didn't hear you. What did you say?" As long as it is a question, it will beg an answer which will adequately engage the brain long enough for you to act. I also try not to ask a question that can be answered 'yes' or 'no', i.e. 'Can we talk about this?' Questions like this do not engage the brain as well as a question that demands a longer answer, i.e. 'What are you trying to say?'

One thing is certain, the longer you take to 'act' the graver the situation becomes, especially when faced with more than one antagonist, time is of the essence, don't waste even a second.

In summary

Once you have put up the fence and lined-up the antagonist with your chosen technique (this should be done within the first seconds of any confrontation) and you are sure that an attack upon your person is imminent, utilise the response sequence previously detailed. If you have to attack, distract and engage his brain with your chosen trigger sentence then, if no other option is open to you, pre-emptively strike from your pre-cocked 'line-up' position. Your engaging verbal should veil your attack. It's very easy here to start getting lost in the explanation of what is occurring. The bottom line is, if you have no other option open to you, ask the assailant a question, hit him whilst his brain is engaged and then run away. It's that simple.

Chapter Four

The Knock Out

Everyone talks about the knock out merchant with reverence because very few fighters seem to be able to achieve the elusive KO. When you talk about knocking out an opponent people often look at you as though you are talking about the impossible. That's because they don't have the knowledge. With the right information and bags of courage the KO is very attainable.

There are many contributing factors that combine and intermingle to form a knock out on an adversary. The most important factor is not, as you might imagine, a powerful strike, but an accurate one. A powerful attack that is not accurate is very unlikely to knock an adversary out. Neither is it a matter of being big or heavy – size is irrelevant. An 8 stone woman who punches her weight will have no trouble knocking a much larger adversary unconscious, if she is accurate.

The next most important factor to accuracy in achieving a KO, is deception. The adversary who does not expect the punch cannot prepare for the punch, therefore the impetus of the punch is maximised. To attain a KO you rely heavily on the looseness of the adversary's neck and jaw muscles, if they are not braced when you strike the jaw, a huge shaking of the adversary's brain will occur, it is this shaking of the brain that will cause unconsciousness. If, however, the adversary sees the strike coming, he will brace himself and thereby minimise the shaking, consequently unconsciousness does not occur so readily.

Verbal disarmament and brain-engagement are pivotal in the execution of an effective KO. The 'fence' allows you to utilise your entire body weight from a stable, balanced posture whilst your verbal, mental disarmament engages the adversary's brain for a split second – this is your window of entry to launch a pre-emptive attack. While the brain is engaged, even for a second, the adversary will not see the punch/ attack coming. Because he doesn't see it coming, he does not brace himself for the strike; the jaw and neck muscles are relaxed, maximum shaking of the brain occurs followed closely by unconsciousness. Also, brain-engagement will cancel out any spontaneous response that your antagonist may have in-built. He will not react during brain engagement. For the same reason (as mentioned in Chapter Two), attacks that are launched outside tunnel vision also have a great effect – the attacker does not see, so cannot prepare for them.

For best results you should strike the jawbone anywhere from the ear to the chin, if struck correctly this will cause the aforementioned shaking of the brain that brings on unconsciousness. If you strike by the ear this will cause minimal shaking of the brain and a short spell of unconsciousness. The further down the jaw you strike the bigger the 'brain shake' and the greater the probability of unconsciousness (also, if unconsciousness does occur it will increase the spell of unconsciousness). By the same count, the further down the jaw you strike the smaller the target area becomes.

A punch on the point of the jaw will have maximum effect but holds the smallest target. The jawbone when struck along the jaw line causes a shaking of the brain. However, when it is struck on the point of the chin the knock out occurs in two phases. First the clivius and the anterior edge of the occipital bone are pushed against the lower portions of the pons and the anterior surface of the medula oblongata. Next, by virtue of the 're-bounding effect', the medula oblongata bounces back against the internal surface of the occipital bone and the posterior edge of the foremen magnum. In essence, the double impact causes the medula oblongata, the most sensitive part of the brain, to concuss, thus causing temporary cancellation of the functions of the central nervous system.

The Fence

The Apple Tree Hypothesis

The chances of such a strike are lessened by the fact that the target is only about one inch in diameter. I call it the 'Apple Tree' hypothesis: if you shake an apple tree at the base of it's trunk, heavy shaking of the upper branches will occur, and lots of apples will fall. If, however, you shake the tree high up the trunk, minimal shaking of the upper branches will occur, and very few apples will fall. It is recommended, therefore, that you aim your blow at the middle of the jaw line (on the curve), where the target area is larger and the effect of an accurate blow will cause unconsciousness of a reasonable duration, certainly long enough to effect escape.

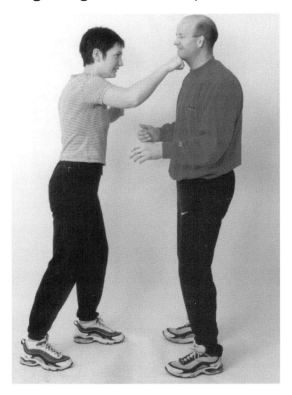

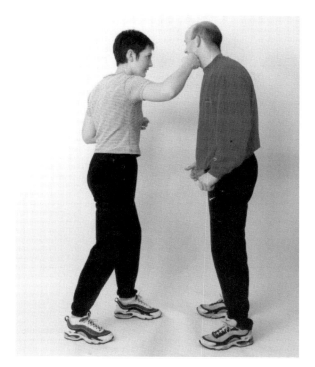

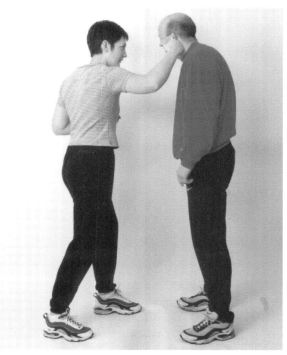

The Fence

The first thing to do, before you strike, is look at the target area on the jaw, if you do not, you are not likely to hit it. When you strike, do so with your best technique, preferably off the back leg to ensure maximum body weight utilisation. (An experienced fighter may throw the technique off his front leg). Don't stop the punch and merely strike the target, punch through it with your blow and your body weight. (There is a school of thought that says punching off the back leg is telegraphed and slower than punching off the front. Let me tell you that the time difference between punching off the back and the front leg would not register on a normal clock, we are talking about a difference of a split second. So, attacking off the front leg may be quicker, but the difference could not be seen by the naked eye.) Speed of punch is not the major factor anyway: I know slow punchers that get KO's in every encounter because they are so good at engaging the brain before attack. Whilst the brain is engaged time stops for the opponent, probably for split second, this is the window of entry for your attack. If time stands still for a second your attack need only be as quick as that and you are in.

A direct hit will cause unconsciousness in an adversary immediately, his fall will then add to his defeat, because the unconscious head will usually meet the floor very heavily. If you are on target, but not right on the button, your adversary will, likely as not, fall to the floor in a semi-conscious stupor from which he usually recovers quite quickly, so get away as soon as possible. Even a blow that is off-target should at least stun the adversary giving you enough time to run. As a matter of course, always try to verbally/ mentally disarm and engage the adversary before you strike, this will greatly enhance the chances of a KO. I would always, when possible, advise you to use a punching technique as opposed to anything else, because the hands are economical, fast and usually closer to the target (jaw), than most other attacking tools. When using the fist to strike, for best effect, strike the line of the jaw with the two major knuckles. If you cannot or do not use the fist then make sure you use the hardest part of whatever attacking tool you do use. 'Bone to bone' is always most effective. You may attack the jaw underneath (uppercut), around (hook), straight (cross), or over hand (hook), depending upon your preferences and strengths. All of these approaches will have the desired effect if accurate, though hooking punches seem to be the most effective.

In summary
1. Line up your adversary using 'fence' to control range and trigger attack
2. Look at the jaw
3. Mentally disarm him and engage the brain, using your verbal action trigger
4. Strike
5. Escape

Chapter Five

Attacking Off The Fence

The sheer control of the fence allows you valuable seconds in the very early stages of a confrontation to assess a situation and decide your options. Should you eclipse the guy, try to talk him down or attempt to run for your life? It is not my right to tell you what you should do, only to offer up the possible options. Your instinct (what we like to call the 'second attention'), should also, if sharp, inform you of your options – if it does, listen to your instinct over everyone else. However, we are not the hunter-gatherers that we once were and our instincts have been blunted somewhat, very often they will send you the wrong information. Frequently, they do send the right information but we, as a race that rely more on exterior information, do not listen, or we listen but do not believe, or we listen and believe but still do not act because our survival mechanisms are rusted from under use. They do say, after all, that if you don't use it (whatever 'it' may be) you lose it. I have found this to be true.

By training under pressure, Animal Day and the like, we are oiling our survival techniques and taking them for a spin. These instincts, like the skeletal muscle, like the brain and not unlike most things in this mechanical existence, will atrophy if they are not used regularly. Although we no longer need to hunt for food and gather berries or fruit, there is still a threat. This threat comes from our own race now as opposed to other animals competing on the food chain – so we need to exercise natural instinct. Our mammalian ancestors would have had more practice than was necessary from the sabre-toothed tiger and other such adversarial creatures. However, because we are out of practise, we have to find another way of sharpening our warrior tools, so that when today's version of the same tiger attacks us outside the chippy, we do not find ourselves grasping for an instinct that has become a metaphoric couch potato. So get the turbo out of the garage and give it a run now and then, just to stop the working parts from rusting over.

The fence allows you the control – not for long mind you – to be able to choose the best option according to what you have been given. As I have said, if your survival instincts are oiled and ready from constant use your second attention will tell you when it is right to run and when it is right to fight. If they are rusted up (more often than not the case), all you will feel is the downward spiral of confusion, doubt and indecision. You are out of the fight before you are even in it.

If you find it necessary to initiate a pre-emptive strike, then attack off the fence. What you use as an attacking tool is your personal choice and there is no one best strike that I can tell you here other than the most available attack on the day. Again, because most people are so out of touch with natural instinct, the second attention, they will not 'feel' what the right technique should be and end up falling into indoctrination (the techniques that your teacher has taught you). What I will say however is that out of necessity it is best to employ your strongest, most comfortable attack. There is nothing to gain and everything to lose if you throw anything less.

The attack is your chosen main artillery technique and whilst many techniques should be practised and perfected throughout your training, one or two, the ones that work best for you, should be taken to one side and isolated – these will be the techniques used in your sniper option. Note: I know at this point there will be those amongst us that say we should be spontaneous and 'go with the flow', react to our attackers, let our chi take over etc. and there are times when this does occur.

I've found myself in situations where I have automatically reacted, almost as though I were outside of my own body, and executed the right techniques for the given situation. I did this more by accident than design and whilst I'd love to be able to do this at will, I can't (I haven't yet met anyone who can). Until I am able to react automatically with the correct response to every scenario, for survival, if nothing else, I will use the method that has taken me successfully through over 300 fights. I have a plan of action and I respond (a conscious, decision-making act) as opposed to react (an unconscious act not involving decision-making). I have a fight plan that I always use and a support system that I can fall back on if all else fails. Whilst many other martial artists – most of these without any 'real' experience – tell me that this is the wrong way, I know that after working it clinically and simply in hundreds of situations that it is correct. I am not alone either: all of the many students that I have taught over the years have worked it as well, if not better than me.

I always plan the first strike. My awareness and perception allows me to do this. I have a profound understanding of today's enemy and I know how to work him. I also have a learned to understand myself and my art – especially what is of use and what is useless. These together allow me to plan a strategy before battle and stop most situations before they really get started. What I will say is that, once the first punch has been thrown – hopefully by me – the rest will be spontaneous, every other shot thrown will be automatic, and to train for this is entirely separate to training for match fighting, 3 second fighting and self-defence. This of course is outside the context of this very exact text. Also worth mentioning is the fact that unless you are fighting against more than one assailant,

The Fence

a 3 second fight, or an ambush fight that goes beyond a few seconds without a result will fall into the category of 'match fighting'. If you are facing multiple attackers, then the chances are that it will become a mascara unless you are highly skilled or extremely lucky.

Main artillery attacking techniques

There is no sense in beating about the bush and saying that main artillery techniques can be taken from any range, because I don't believe that they can. If punching range is the one most often given in a real situation, then that is where the main artillery should be drawn from. Having said that I always think it is wise to have one or two very strong techniques at every range, after all a chain is only as strong as its weakest link.

Hand Techniques

These are the order of the day, and there is little point in manufacturing another range when the one you are already in – or most likely to be in – is the most clinical anyway. Kicking and grappling ranges are far from clinical. They are, at best, elongated ranges where it usually takes several blows or seconds to finish an adversary as opposed to the split second it can take to finish a fight with a good hand technique. This is not to say that I don't rate these other worthy ranges, I spend many hours perfecting them for my own artillery, but in the support as opposed to at the front line. I know that the grappling fans out there will already be disagreeing with me here because it has already been proven that grappling, especially Ne-waza (ground fighting), is potentate in the open match fighting arena. I agree wholeheartedly. However, we are not talking about a one on one match fight scenario – we are talking about a fight that will explode in your face at the bar of a pub or the counter of a chip shop. We are talking about several potential opponents who will devour you should you dare take the fight down to the ground.

In all of the thousands of street attacks and fights that I have witnessed, hardly any were match fights or became match fights. Most were over as quickly as they began. Many of the fights that did go to the ground usually turned out very badly for the person that was outnumbered. Two of my friends were badly stabbed, in separate incidents, when they took the fight to the floor: one was stabbed by the girlfriend of his opponent; the other by the mother of his opponent. I have also known of several men who were doing well on the floor and then got kicked, literally, to death by the friends of their opponent. So there is a time and a place for grappling, and in its time and place I would bet my house on the grappler winning, but out of context it is out of its depth.

The Fence

Kicking Range

Firstly you rarely have the range, secondly when you do it is gobbled up by a greedy aggressor that will be in your face before you get your foot of the floor. The best time to kick an opponent is when he falls over. The rest of the time the feet are best employed for balance or making a hasty retreat when you are outnumbered or out-gunned. No offence intended to either kickers or grapplers. This is my truth as I see it from the inside!

Punching Range

Punching range is a very mobile range. An expert puncher can move through several opponents in as many seconds, this would be very difficult with kicking range – kicks are better employed as a finishing technique to a prostrate opponent – and almost impossible with grappling range – which is better suited to the match fight scenario.

One of my favourite punchers, Owen, regularly tore up malevolents like tissue at a snot party, and always with his hands. He weighed less that 10 stone but when he punched your ancestors felt it. Once, on holiday in Spain he was harassed by two huge German fellows, who kept taking the piss out of the fact that he had big ears. (I have to say that his ears are worthy of a good piss-take, but didn't they know that we won the war.) Finally he had enough of their malicious banter and told them so. They did not take kindly to this and squared up to the little fellow.

'BANG! BANG!'

Two clinical punches later the two German lads were as one with the carpet. Owen went back to his beer. Winston was the same, he was so good with his hands that I always felt like the lad was carrying a gun. He was an awesome pugilist. When he put his hands on you it was like an overdose of sleeping pills. John could throw a mean punch too. The other lads used to call him Horlicks because, on the door, he used to put people to sleep last thing at night. I'm digressing, not like me I know, but I am trying to get the point across that, given the present environment and the contemporary enemy, 'hands' are the order of the day.

I will list a few techniques that I use but, basically, any short-range technique, preferably hand technique (as long as it is a finishing technique) will suffice. I would keep clear of time wasting and superfluous techniques – anything flashy or flicky should go back in the lucky bag with the other plastic toys. Once you get this far into an altercation you may have one chance and one chance only – don't waste it – once the opportunity has gone it may never present itself again. Your attack should be a destroying technique that hits your opponent like a steam train, not a silly-flicky back fist that might make his eyes water, (if you want to do that you'd be better employed reading him an extract from *Love Story*).

The Fence

Trapping/ jamming and the like have their place, but again are also unlikely to have any relevance here – unless your opponent touches, grabs or points, then a basic trap can be followed by a devastating head butt or hand strike. If you hold your fence correctly however, it becomes very difficult for anyone to do this. Once a fight becomes live nothing stays still for long and the concept of flowing through a series of fancy movements is not a sound one. If you beg to differ, then I respect your opinion but please don't try and convince me. Have an Animal Day (a training session where the participants fight all out with very few rules and any range is allowed) at your own club and see for yourself. When you watch someone like the brilliant Rick Young teach trapping it makes you realise what a valid part of your armoury it can be, but, even Rick will probably tell you, it is an incidental range used to back up main artillery technique. Basic trapping therefore is a valid – though very small – part of the support system. A fight goes from talking distance to 'in your face' in the blink of a eye.

People often ask me what is the best means of physical defence and I always reply, 'learn to hit fucking hard', and that's the bottom line. Learn how to hit very very hard and you'll come out of most situations on top. But please learn to do it from the right range: it's one thing being able to hit hard from a comfortable range and from a guard position or perhaps even using combination to build momentum and power, but how well will you fare when the distance you are used to is halved and you have to punch from a no-guard position? It's a completely different ball game, so it is important to train your techniques as close to reality as possible, so that when you make the step from dojo to street that step is not such a big one. If you are used to compliance in training you've got a very big shock coming to you when the proverbial shit hits the fan.

In the vast majority of situations I have been involved in, I have used a left lead 'fence' to set up a right handed punch – sometimes a cross, sometimes a hook. My base is usually always a very small left lead forty-five degree stance, and I always ask a question before I strike to trigger my action and to engage the opponent's brain. Other people I have worked with prefer a left lead stance and a right hand fence, punching with a left hook off the lead leg. Others still favour a left lead fence from a left lead stance and attacked with a pummelling head butt. For those that prefer the lead hand or reverse hand finger strike is also a good 'stopping technique'.

It is worth remembering that your opponent will be experiencing tunnel vision as a by-product of adrenal reaction. In real terms this means that by placing your attacking hand, left or right, slightly outside of his tunnel vision you can strike him without him seeing

The Fence

the blow. That's why hook punches very often KO people, because they come from outside tunnel vision.

Brain engagement

To maximise KO potential, always ask the opponent a question before you attack, it engages the brain giving you a blind second before attack. It also acts a nice action trigger for the attack. It doesn't matter what you ask as long as it engages the brain.

Here are a few of the more common 'line-up' techniques taken from a fence:

Right Cross/Hook

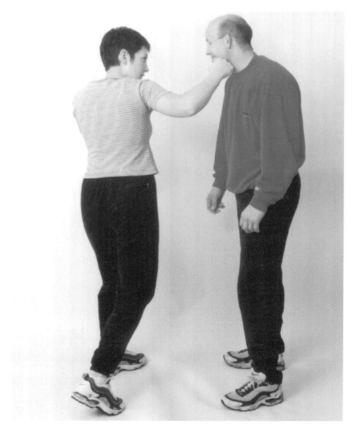

Thrown from the rear of a left-leading stance can be tremendously powerful and effective. Its only real infirmity is that, because it is thrown from the rear leg, it can be slightly telegraphed. From a right-lead stance this technique may be executed using the left-hand.

Left Hook

Thrown from the front leg of a left-lead stance. If employed by a 'practised' pugilist, this punch can be very destructive. Because it is thrown from the front leg it is less telegraphed than other techniques and it has less distance to travel to the target. Because of the high skill factor involved it is not a recommended punch for the novice.

The Fence

Head Butt

A very 'pain inflicting' attack, usually directed at the opponent's nose. If executed correctly utilising the body weight it can cause enormous damage to an adversary, though it is not known as a knock out technique.

Elbow

If you find yourself very close to the opponent, then an elbow may be the best available technique. Use the left hand as 'fence' and smash the right elbow into the chest or face of the opponent.

Off Centring The Opponent

With hand strikes from a right lead fence you have the option, should you care to take it, to off centre the opponent before you attack him. This adds to the effect of your attack when you launch it. It also has the added effect of opening up the potential target area, the jaw, before the attack. The effect of the attack is more potent because at the moment of impact the opponent is off balance. I off centre the opponent by stepping to the right with my right foot before I attack, I disguise the step or movement with dialogue.

Finger Jab

The finger jab is what Bruce Lee would have called the most dangerous technique available. You can attack using the left hand or the right, preferably from a passive fence, which in any language in the world says 'I don't want trouble'. This is good because the opponent will think that you are already defeated and mentally drop his guard. Strike fast and sharp, up the face and into the eyes as opposed to directly at the eyes. Again, if you attack directly at the eyes, there's a fair chance that the opponent will automatically retract to defend. If you attack up the face and into the eyes the attack comes from outside tunnel vision, so he won't see it and you are more likely to have a result.

If you do attack the eyes please don't kid yourself as to the result of your attack. All eye attacks are very serious and a direct strike with even a small amount of force may blind an opponent for life. Which is OK if that's what you feel you need to do to save your life, but not so clever if you are just scrapping around in the garden with your next door neighbour Johnny!

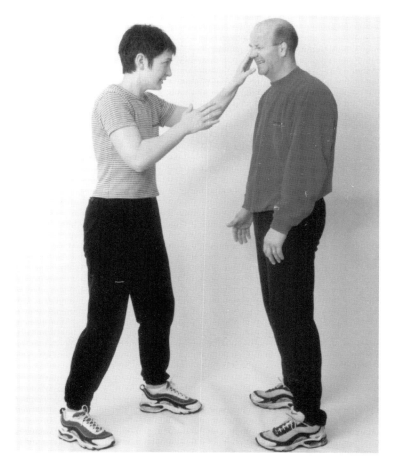

The Fence

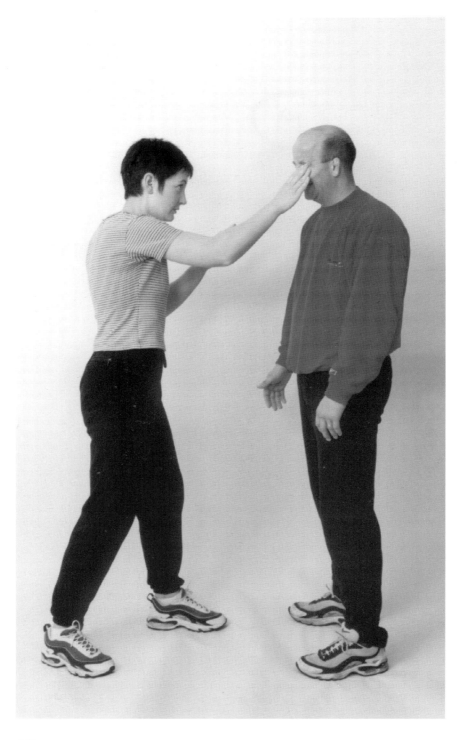

Chapter Six

The Mr R Method

Mr R was an expert with the head and destroyed many opponents with the said technique. He usually worked with a wide, natural fence and used a whiplashing butt that left most opponents thinking that they were cabbages.

The Fence

If the threat was very high Mr R would employ the passive fence and attack with the front of the head thus;

Chapter Seven

The Mr H Method

Mr H was the master of line-up and would often use submissive verbal to talk his way into an attack that very few survived. I once watched him use this to effect seven times in one night with seven KO's and, believe it or not, every single one of them left him with no other choice. He tried to give them all a way out but none took it, so were carried out instead. What he always did was to use verbal dissuasion to try and talk his opponents down, at the same time he would off centre them by taking their lead elbow with his left hand. This would be done in such a gentle way that his opponents never sensed his intent. If at any point during the exercise they showed any resistance or aggression he would strike from wherever he was and end the altercation on the spot. Also, if the verbal dissuasion worked and they were willing to talk he would not attack and let them go on their merry little way none the wiser.

Notice from the illustrations how Mr H neutralises his opponent's right arm by gripping his elbow with his left, and neutralises his right hand and balance by off-centering them. Also by off-centering his opponent he opens their face area for the potential of huge attack.

The Fence

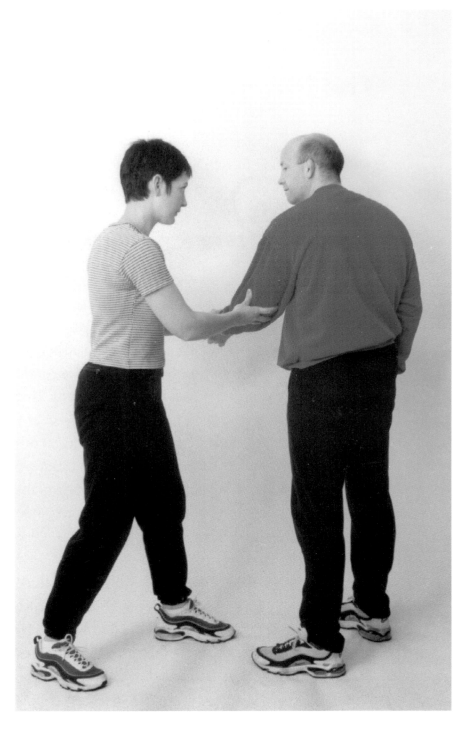

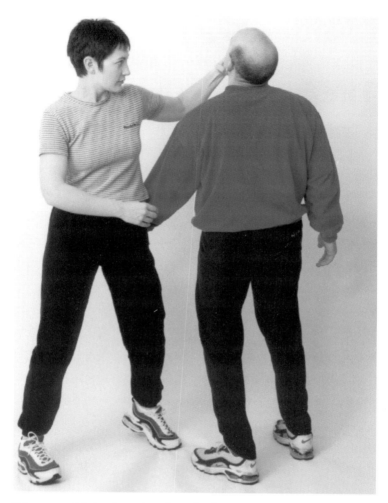

The sensitivity involved with this, and all areas of fence work, is amazing. Once you become practised with it you can feel the energy of the opponent, you can read his intentions, you learn to feel whether he is a threat or a mouth, and deal with him accordingly. It is very hard to get that across via photos in a book, but hopefully with practice you will feel it. When I'm on the street I feel protected because of the knowledge that I have of the fence. I hope you will too.

The Fence

Chapter Eight

The Mr G Method

Mr G is the friend of mine, the one that the other doormen used to call Horlicks (because he put people to sleep last thing at night). He was an awesome puncher with a very unorthodox, but highly proficient, method of attacking with either hand – a prolific KO merchant and only about 10 stone at his best.

His method entailed waiting until he had no option available to him other than a physical response, whereupon he would unleash an almighty right or left hand punch that had a 95% KO rate. What made his method unorthodox, and therefore worth looking at, was the fact that he used an invisible fence (not so unusual in itself) and he always ducked before he threw his attack. When he first showed me how he worked I wondered how he got away with such a large movement before he attacked but on closer examination I could see that the duck before his attack actually helped prime his opponent. One minute his was in front of them, the next – only for a split second before he eclipsed them – he was gone. He actually ducked under their eye-line, which completely flummoxed them. When he re-emerged he used the bounce from the bend to ensure massive momentum in his chosen strike.

The illustrations demonstrate his method better than my words can. I know in the pictures it all looks a little telegraphed, but believe me when I tell you that this 10 stoner knocked out some of the best and biggest fighters in the city with this very technique – he had it down to a fine art. Like the others this technique is very linear. The characteristics of these techniques are that they all take a very short and direct route to the target, they are all extremely explosive and come from a very short range (conversation range in fact) and they are all, without exception, pre-emptive.

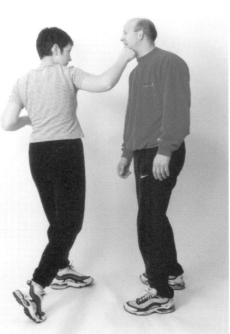

Chapter Nine

The Thompson Method

My own method, I have to say, does vary according to the situation and, at one time or another, I have used all of the techniques described herein to effect. However the greater majority of my line-ups were either right hooks or right crosses using a left hand fence, right hand attack. I always worked from very short range and always attacked first, if I couldn't talk my way out of a physical response. I am not as experienced as Mr T or Mr Anderson but I did have over 50 KO's with this method and it is the method that I still employ today.

I take up a fence as soon as the situation touches conversation range, this is generally straight away. From my experience people that want to argue/fight do not usually do it from a distance, if they did there would be no real threat as you could just turn and walk away. The fence is 95% of what I do, I control from the first second that the threat arises until my opponent is unconscious or controlled or I have escaped. I employ the fence on a very subtle level so that the opponent is unaware of my control, all he knows is – and this is not on a conscious level – that the gap between he and I is blocked and there is no thoroughfare for his attacking tools.

I allow my hands to hover a little so that I can pre-emptively trap and stop his right and left hands. I am extremely sensitive to his body movement, so that he is unable to butt, kick or knee me. If he moves even a fraction I check him with my fence. I stay in a small forty five degree stance to maintain balance and allow me a strong platform from which to attack. Very often I off-centre my opponents before I attack (if I think this will help my cause). Usually I will check behind my attacker (I'm not recommending this, it's just something that I felt comfortable with) to see where he was going to fall when I hit him. If I was in a bar and there was a table full of innocent people drinking at the table I would alter my attack, or the angle of attack, so that my opponent didn't fall into the table and hurt these people. If the table was full of his friends, people that I knew would attack me as soon as the fight kicked off, then I might deliver my blow so that he did fall into the table and injure them, and himself of course. If I was in the street and my opponent had his back to a busy road, I might not want to send him spiralling into heavy traffic, therefore I would alter the angle of my blow so that he fell on the spot or to the side, as opposed to backwards. Equally, if he was side-on to the road I might change the angle of my blow so that he fell backwards, i.e. onto the pavement and not sideways onto the road and into the traffic.

The Fence

You might find this all ridiculous, after all why should we be benevolent to someone that has chosen to attack us for no reason? Personally, I don't want to kill anyone because it is not in my nature. Secondly, and equally as important: if I kill another person then there is a great probability that I am going to jail for a long time, not an experience that I want to add to my CV.

I reiterate that as an experienced fighter I could quite often alter the angle of my opponent's fall – but not always – sometimes it wasn't possible because I felt the threat was too great. If you are inexperienced you'd be foolhardy to attempt this, because that moment of contemplation could create an attacking window for your opponent to climb through. Believe me when I tell you that your opponent will not be thinking about the consequences of punching you into a table of drinks or heavy traffic. I include it in here simply because it is a part of my method.

The way I control the fall of the attacker is by changing the angle of my punch. If I hit them very heavily with a straight punch, on the point of the jaw they are likely to go out and back. If however I throw the same straight punch but clip down on the jaw at the last second, I will get a KO, because the clipping punch will shake the brain, but will not drive the opponent backwards – rather he will fall on the spot.

With a hook punch it is slightly different, as anyone with KO experience will agree. For instance a driving right hook to the jaw, which in theory should knock the opponent out and send him spiralling to the left, does just the opposite. Usually the opponent falls flat where they were standing (their head generally hits the floor where their feet were) or even the opposite way, quite often falling straight into you. This can be dangerous if they are not completely out because, in their panic they can grab you and end up in a grappling match.

The great danger with the driving hook is that the opponent falls like a slaughtered cow and their head smashes heavily onto the floor. If they are going to die as a consequence of your attack this is what usually always does it. If you clip the jaw with a downward hook as opposed to a driving hook you can lessen the intensity of the fall. With the downward clip they still fall unconscious but not so deeply, the fall then tends to be a tumble as opposed to a crashing fall.

Before my attack I always ask a question to engage the brain, this gives me the blind second I require to allow my attack to enter unhindered. The fact that the brain is engaged also heightens the probability of a KO because it is the punch that isn't seen/perceived that does the most damage. The question also acts as an action trigger, when I ask the question that's it – the punch is on its way. This is the way I train and this

The Fence

is the way that I fight. I always aim for the jawbone, usually about half way down between the ear and the point of the jaw. If the first attack does not do the job, then I automatically fall into the support system and attack with techniques that fit the energy that he gives me. From here on in it will all fall into spontaneity and again I will react according to the way I have trained. If I have trained for semi-contact, the blow-pulling point-scoring stuff, then that is what I will get when things go auto. Again, unless you are very good at controlling vertical fighting, specifically the scruffy variety, you will end up on the floor so a sound knowledge of that arena is what you'll need to survive.

Here are some illustrations of my method, feel free to tailor it so that it fits you.

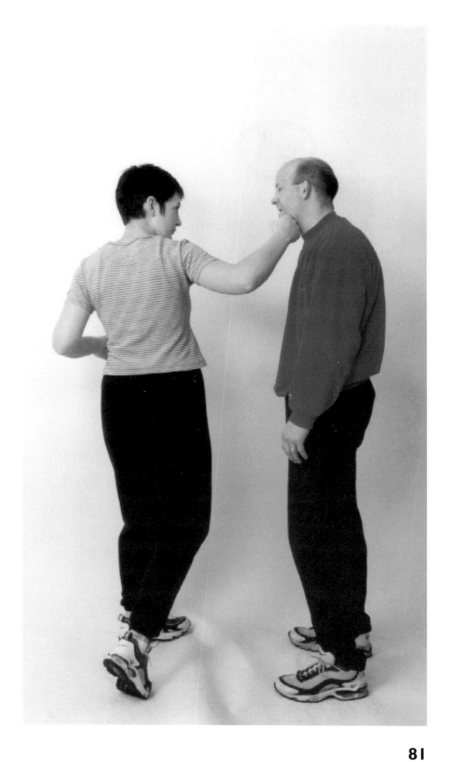

Chapter Ten

The Mr Briggs Method

Mr Briggs prefers the slap, in fact he has it down to a fine art. Taken from the teachings of the 'double hip' master Mr Peter Consterdine (actually Peter's getting on a bit now and it has become more of a dodgy hip that a double hip), Mr Briggs has made the technique his own. The reason I like this method is because of the unusual nature of the fence that he employs. Mr Briggs had 15 KO's in live scenarios last year alone with this technique.

Working from a 45 degree stance, The Briggs method entails pushing the left elbow forward and placing the left hand by the ear, as though trying to listen to what the opponent has to say. This is especially effective in close environments where there is a lot of noise like a pub or a nightclub. You will see from the picture how natural this looks. The elbow works innocently as a blocking fence. The right hand, the attacking hand, splays out in exclamation and he then uses the brain engaging, action triggering statement that fits with the pose, 'sorry what did you say'. From here you attack in a close hooking motion and slap or palm heel to the jaw or ear for the KO. Short, sharp and ferocious.

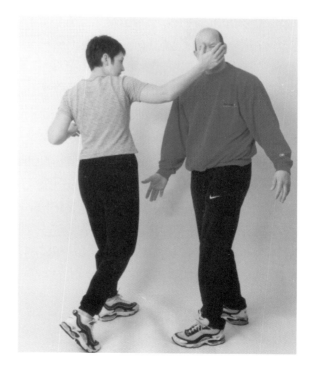

Chapter Eleven

The Mr T Method

Mr T, to my knowledge, was in over 500 fights over a fifteen year period and was probably the most prolific Judas-merchant I have ever encountered. Lovely hands but a master in the art of pre-fight deception. I could probably fill a book with his techniques alone. However, I haven't the room so I'll take the one that I like most and that he employed to great effect on so many occasions. I like to call it the sliding elbow technique. This is specifically for situations where you have a ledge at elbow height to lean on.

This technique incorporates leaning very lightly on a bar with your attacking arm, in this case the left arm and using the right hand as fence. This is a very dangerous situation because of the very close proximity, so caution and great sensitivity is called for. Control the gap with the right hand fence, lay the left elbow on the bar, this gives it the effect of being redundant as an attacking tool, so the opponent will take very little notice of it. The left hand will fall just outside the tunnel of vision, so when you do attack with it you'll get maximum effect, because it will not be seen, only felt.

As and when you feel an attack is called for (only you can know for sure when the time is right), ask a question to engage the brain and then attack with a left hook or slap, sliding the attacking arm sharply off the bar and driving your hips through at the end of the technique, to ensure power and depth of attack. This is an advanced technique and should not be considered unless you have an excellent lead hand left hook.

Note: we didn't have a bar in the photo studio, so please try and use your imagination and see a 'bar' under the left elbow of the attacker.

Chapter Twelve

The Mr Anderson Method

As far as modern combatants go Mr Anderson, my teacher in things real, is the master. Although he was innately well-versed in different ranges he specialised, like all the greats that I worked with, in hands, specifically the left hook. I think it is worth mentioning that Mr Anderson – who you can read about extensively in my three autobiographical books *Watch My Back, Bouncer* and *On The Door* – was not formerly trained in any fighting art. All of his knowledge has been learned in the field as it were. Again his technique is unusual in that he uses a left, lead hand fence and a left lead hand hook as the attacking tool. This is very specialist and should not be undertaken unless your short range punching power is top notch.

The Anderson method incorporates using the left hand (fence) to feel out the potential attacker's intentions. If your opponent touches the fence, then he is trying to bridge the gap. If he is trying to bridge the gap, this being a precursor in the attack ritual to actual attack, then he is preparing for assault. Mr Anderson would gently push the antagonist back with his left hand to check out their intentions. If they were posturing and not fighting, then they would stay back out of range and therefore no longer be a threat. If their intentions were violent then they would aggressively push back to make up the lost space. At this point Mr Anderson would hit them with a left hook that few, none that I ever saw, would survive. As he attacked he would step slightly across with his lead left leg and drive the punch through. Add to this the fact that his opponent would be moving onto the attack and you have the recipe for a KO. His attack was extremely short range, probably moving only six inches to a foot before contact.

The illustrations will show you better how the Anderson Method works. Timing is important here because he is attacking as the opponent moves forward. A second out and you will miss, losing possibly your one and only opportunity.

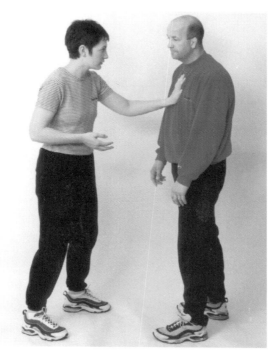

Chapter Thirteen

Kicking Off The Fence

If I kick off the fence – I very rarely do – I will only do it as a part of posturing, that is, to psyche the opponent out. I will use the kick as a minimal attack to trigger adrenal dump, and hopefully capitulation, in my opponent. If I kick it will generally be very low, groin and downward. The Thai leg kick is my ideal choice because it not only triggers adrenaline it also partly disables the fighter, so that if he does decide to 'have a go' he will be doing so with half of his armoury lost.

If you decide that this is the option for you, make sure that you know what you are opening yourself up to. If you try to use the kick as a finishing technique you could be in trouble because it very rarely works, and if the guy is strong and overrides the attack you are in for a match fight. Only use the kick if you sense that the opponent will fall for the posturing ploy, and immediately after the kick make sure that you create a gap between you and him, to trigger his 'flight response'. Make the attack your very best effort, anything less and you may not trigger adrenal dump and therefore not get the desired response

Chapter Fourteen

Choking Off The Fence

The spin and choke off the fence is a technique I used when I felt that a restraint was viable. Note: I have never tried to restrain someone that was a high-risk threat, it would be too dangerous. Only use this if the threat is low risk and you feel you can get away with it.

The illustrations will show the spin and choke a lot better than I can describe here, but basically I would work off a staggered fence. When I felt the threat was beyond dissuasion I would ask a question to engage the opponent's brain and then sharply push his left shoulder with my right hand and pull his right shoulder with my left hand, spinning him so that his back was to my chest. I would then wrap my right arm around his neck and couple up with my left to make the choke. From here you have the option – and this will be determined by how the opponent reacts – to talk him down using the choke as leverage to persuade him, or choke him out if he persists in being violent. If you are working in security you also have the option of dragging him off the premises using the choke.

Beware: this is a highly dangerous technique that should always be used with great care – many have been choked to death, usually by accident, with this technique. Practice it in the controlled arena until you have the control to employ it in a tempered manner. Of course there are more ways to choke or restrain off the fence, this is just an appetiser to give you direction should you prefer to restrain as opposed to attack.

The Fence

Conclusion

As a final point on attack, don't ever pull your technique. If a situation has become so bad that you are forced to hit someone to protect yourself then they deserve everything they get – pulling your technique is the quickest way to the graveyard. So either attack all-out or do not attack at all. The only exception to this rule is if you are very experienced and feel you can judge the potency of your attacker. I was often faced with people that were not enough of a threat to demand a good hiding, but enough of a threat to be dangerous, so I would use an adrenaline switch (posturing) to psyche them out and thus beat them without coming to arms. This requires a lot of discernment, so unless you are very experienced don't take the chance.

It is also my recommendation that, once you have hit your opponent, you make good your escape. This might not be how you see fighting, but it is good self-defence. The only time you need to 'finish off' an opponent is when he is still a threat, if he is not then there is no need, (I realise that this contradicts some of the things I have said in *Watch My Back, Bouncer* and *On The Door*, but bouncing is a different arena where many rules have to be broken to keep the peace long term). I have seen many people go for a finish, when a finish was not necessary, losing as a consequence because their attackers have grabbed them. Use the distraction of your attack to make good an escape – that is my advice if the situation is one of self-defence. Also don't forget environmental fences like tables and chairs. If you are in your car that can also act as a fence if you lock the doors – in fact it is about 3000lbs worth of fence.

If you ever find yourself in a situation where you are restraining one opponent and are approached by a second, use the one you are restraining as a fence by facing him towards the second potential attacker. If No. 2 persists slam No. 1 to the floor between you and No. 2, again as a fence. There are many ways of using your natural surroundings as a fence, use your imagination, and as long as it gets you out of a bad situation and it doesn't harm innocent people then use it.

Make the fence your own with diligent practice and you will be a lot safer when violence comes a calling – and it will find you wherever you are – or face the potential of going into battle with no main artillery.

Good luck, keep training and be a nice person. God bless.

Geoff Thompson, 1998